SO-ATV-734

ACTION

JOB SKILLS

How to Act Right on the Job

M.G. HIGGINS

LIFESKILLS IN ACTION
JOB SKILLS

MONEY

Living on a Budget | Road Trip
Opening a Bank Account | The Guitar
Managing Credit | High Cost
Using Coupons | Get the Deal
Planning to Save | Something Big

LIVING

Smart Grocery Shopping | Shop Smart
Doing Household Chores | Keep It Clean
Finding a Place to Live | A Place of Our Own
Moving In | Pack Up
Cooking Your Own Meals | Dinner Is Served

JOB

Preparing a Resume | Not Her Job
Finding a Job | Dream Jobs
Job Interview Basics | Job Ready
How to Act Right on the Job | Choices
Employee Rights | Not So Sweet

SADDLEBACK
EDUCATIONAL PUBLISHING
www.sdlback.com

All source images from Shutterstock.com

ISBN-13: 978-1-68021-411-6
eBook: 978-1-63078-812-4

Printed in Malaysia

22 21 20 19 18   2 3 4 5 6

Success at a job takes effort.

It is not just showing up.

People must work hard every day.

This shows their value.

It is a big part of **keeping a job**.

The first day at a job is busy.

There are forms to sign.

Your boss will explain pay and benefits.

You may be given a handbook.

It lists the rules.

Handbooks give information about:

- breaks
- holidays
- sick time
- vacation time
- time sheets
- pay dates
- safety
- what to wear

Learning the rules is important.

It helps to know what to expect.

Read the handbook.

Keep it handy.

Look things up as needed.

The company may be small.

Rules might not be written down.

Someone should share them.

Ask if you aren't sure.

There are also **unwritten rules**.

These are how things are done.

They are not official rules.

Pay attention to how people do things.

This will help you succeed.

Some rules apply to all jobs.

One is getting to work on time.

This is big.

Your boss relies on you.

So does the rest of the team.

Always be **on time**.

Sometimes there are emergencies.

Being late can't be helped.

Call your boss right away.

Tell them when you'll be in.

People can get sick too.

Call your boss.

Stay home.

Take care of yourself.

Get well before going back to work.

Don't spread germs.

It's great when work is fun.

But jobs are serious.

You are getting paid to work.

Focus on tasks.

Do personal things on your own time.

Make phone calls during breaks.

Send emails then too.

Breaks are the time for social media.

Work time is not.

Learning a new job takes time.

Tasks may be hard.

There is much to know.

Listen carefully to directions.

Keep a notepad.

Take notes.

These can help later.

Focus on  things.

- What needs to be done
- How to do it
- When it is due

Watch a coworker who does that job.

Get a feel for each step.

Then do the task.

Ask them to watch you.

They can give tips.

Making mistakes is normal.

Try to **learn from them**.

What went wrong?

Think of ways to fix mistakes.

Bosses give **feedback**.

It might be good.

But it won't always be.

Listen to what is said.

Stay calm.

Don't get mad.

Make changes.

This is how people learn.

Mistakes happen.

Work to avoid them.

Focus.

Slow down.

Avoid distractions.

You might need more training.

Ask your boss for help.

Don't give up.

People learn from mistakes.

Skills grow with time.

Jobs are best when people get along.

That means being a good **team player**.

Be friendly.

Help others when you can.

Work hard.

Finish tasks on time.

Be polite.

This makes you easy to work with.

People will like you.

Workers can be very different.

Some may be like you.

Others may not.

Being open-minded is key.

Get to know people.

It will help to understand them.

Many things are good to talk about at work.

Other things are not.

Never gripe about the boss.

Don't complain about the company.

Avoid gossip.

There are other topics to avoid:

- pay

- personal problems

- sex

- religion

- politics

After a while, you may have an **evaluation**.

This is a review of your work.

Often this happens once a year.

The boss thinks about your work.

What is going well?

What could be better?

EVALUATION

Bosses look for other things too.

Do your best every day.

Have a good attitude.

Be confident.

Tell the truth.

Be excited to learn.

Do things without being asked.

Think about how you're doing.

Be ready to talk about this in the meeting.

Think about what your boss said.

Work to **improve**.

Learn new skills.

Ask for new tasks.

Share your ideas.

Work well with others.

Find ways to shine every day.

Many companies offer **raises**.

This might happen once a year.

Your salary will change.

Sometimes this is part of the review.

Other times it is a separate meeting.

You may have to ask for a raise.

Have some facts on hand.

Know what other people in that
job make.

Say what you add to the company.

Your boss will say yes or no.

Be polite either way.

A job may last a few months.

It could last much longer.

There are times people leave jobs.

Do it on good terms.

Tell the boss when you plan to quit.

Give at least **two weeks notice**.

Work hard through your last day.

This is the right thing to do.

The boss will think well of you.

They may give a good reference.

New jobs are fun.

They can be tough too.

Be **patient**.

Work hard.

This leads to success.

What happens when Luke slacks off on the job? Find out in *Choices*. Want to read on?

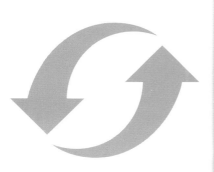

Choices

PJ GRAY

JUST *flip* THE BOOK!

choices

PJ GRAY

LIFESKILLS IN ACTION
JOB SKILLS

SADDLEBACK
EDUCATIONAL PUBLISHING
www.sdlback.com

All source images from Shutterstock.com

ISBN-13: 978-1-68021-411-6
eBook: 978-1-63078-812-4

Printed in Malaysia

22 21 20 19 18   2 3 4 5 6

Jose and Luke work at a travel company. They are on the call center team. People call for help with travel plans. The team books hotel rooms. They schedule flights. Car services are arranged too.

Jose and Luke started on the same day. That was almost a year ago. They sit next to each other. Gina sits on the other side of Luke. She started a few months after they did.

Judy is their boss. She manages the call center. One day Judy stops by Jose's desk. She hands him a paper.

"Nicely done, Jose," Judy says. "This is a letter from a customer. You helped him with a problem. He said that you did a great job."

"Wow," Jose says. "Thank you."

"Keep up the good work."

Luke walks in a moment later. He sets his backpack on his desk. Judy turns to him. "Luke, may I see you in my office?"

Luke and Judy sit in her office. "You are late again," she says.

"I know," Luke says. "I forgot my lunch and had to go back for it."

"Please don't be late again. We are very busy. We need you here on time every day."

"Okay."

"We also need to talk about your clothes."

"What about them?" Luke is wearing a T-shirt and jeans. His jeans have big holes in the knees.

"We have a dress code here," Judy says. "Are you aware of it?"

"Yes," Luke replies.

"We ask that everyone follows the dress code. Check the company handbook."

"What's wrong with my clothes?"

"T-shirts are not allowed," Judy says.

"But jeans are okay," Luke replies.

"Yes, jeans with no holes."

"Okay," Luke says. "I won't wear them again."

"Thank you."

Luke goes back to his desk. He looks over at Jose. "I hate her," Luke says.

Jose does not reply. He turns back to his work.

The next day Luke calls in sick. The office is very busy that day. Jose handles the extra calls.

Gina stops by Jose's desk. "Judy said to take a break," Gina says. "I will cover for you."

"Thanks, Gina."

"I am so mad at Luke," she says.

"Why?"

"We are so busy today," Gina says. "And I know Luke isn't sick."

"How do you know?" Jose asks.

"His friends posted a picture online," she replies. "They are at a ballgame. And Luke is with them."

A few days pass by. It is the end of the month. Reports are due. Every worker must turn one in.

Luke is not good at creating reports. He rushes. His reports have many mistakes. They often get turned in late.

A few days later, Judy asks Luke to her office. She shows Luke his monthly report. "Luke, this is full of mistakes. There are spelling errors all over the place. The numbers don't add up. We have talked about this before. These reports are very important. This is not acceptable."

Luke looks at the report. He says nothing.

"You need to use a spreadsheet with the numbers. And spelling errors will be caught by spell check. These are easy ways for you to be more careful. I would also suggest more training," Judy says.

"I don't need it," Luke replies.

"It really looks like you do. You keep making the same mistakes. I would like to offer you some help."

"What kind of help?"

"I want Jose to train you again. He can show you how he does his reports."

"Why him?" Luke does not like Jose.

"He is very good at his monthly reports. I think he can help you."

"I would rather not," Luke says.

"You should accept the training," Judy says. "I expect next month's report to have no errors."

"It won't," Luke says.

"And it must be turned in on time."

"It will be," he says.

Judy gives Luke a paper. "Please sign this. It states that we talked about this."

Luke signs the paper. Judy adds it to Luke's file.

Another week goes by.

Luke gets a call on his cell phone.

Gina looks over at Luke. Personal calls are not allowed. She hears him say, "Sure. I don't have plans tonight. The party sounds like fun. I'll come by right after work."

A few minutes later, Judy asks the team to her office. "I have a big project that I need some help with. I need it finished today."

Judy looks at each member of the team. "Can anyone stay late to help? I wouldn't ask if it wasn't important."

Jose says, "I will stay."

"Me too," Gina says.

Judy smiles. "Thank you both. You will get overtime pay."

Judy looks at Luke. "Can you help us?"

"No," he says. "I'm going to see my grandmother tonight. She's in the hospital."

Gina looks at Luke and shakes her head. She knows he's going to a party. There is no sick grandmother.

A few weeks go by.

Judy asks Jose to her office. "You have done a great job, Jose."

"Thank you."

"Our customers appreciate you. The other workers do too."

"I enjoy working here very much," Jose replies.

"You are ready for a promotion. Call center manager," Judy says.

"Wow!"

"You have earned it. And it means more pay."

Judy stands up. "Will you take the job?" She offers her hand.

Jose stands and shakes her hand. "Yes. Thank you."

"Great," Judy says. "We will start training next week."

Judy tells the team about Jose's new role. Gina is happy for him. She smiles and says, "You earned it!"

Monday comes. Jose is excited. He goes to Judy's office.

"Good morning! Ready to train me?"

"There is something I have to do," she says. "Please sit down."

Jose sits.

"I hate to start your training with this," Judy says. "It is one of the hardest parts of the job. But it's something a manager must learn. We have to let someone go today."

Jose stops smiling.

Judy opens a file. "This person has not done well. He has had many warnings. But there has been no improvement. I am going to fire him today."

Jose waits for Judy's next words.

"Jose," she says. "I want you with me."

"During the firing?"

"Yes," Judy says. "It is part of your training."

She hands the file to Jose. It is Luke's.

Keeping a job is hard work. Want to learn how to do your best on the job?

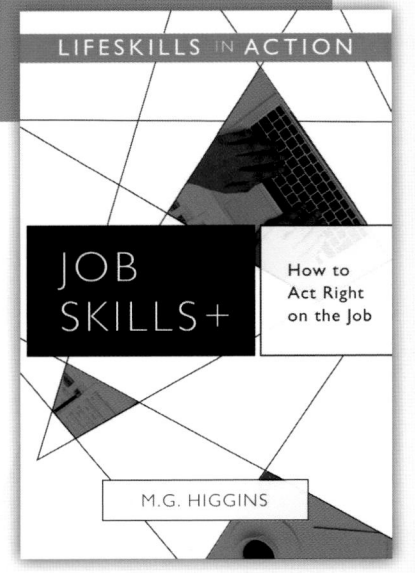

LIFESKILLS IN ACTION

JOB SKILLS+

How to Act Right on the Job

M.G. HIGGINS

JUST *flip* THE BOOK!